Mommy, Who is Donald J. Trump?

By Taffy Jensen

VANALDEN
MEDIA

For my three delicious kids. Who ask
So. Many. Questions.

Printed in the United States of America

Third printing, 2017

Vanalden Media
18960 Ventura Blvd., #95
Tarzana, CA 91356

www.vanaldenmedia.com

Up until 2015, Donald J. Trump was best known as an American businessman and real estate developer.

He was Chairman and President of The Trump Organization, a big company he worked hard to build. He is a billionaire.

Mr. Trump earned his fortune by building and owning properties like hotels, golf courses, offices, and residences, that people pay to use and enjoy.

A **billionaire** has billions of dollars in money and property. Billionaires are very rich and rare.

Mr. Trump had also written many books and starred in his own successful television show.

Mr. Trump starred in "The Apprentice" on NBC from 2004 to 2010. His 1987 book "The Art of the Deal" is one of the best-selling business books of all time.

In addition to being rich, Mr. Trump was famous. He was often featured in newspaper, television, and internet stories.

People were interested in him because he was a successful man with a colorful, outgoing, confident, and often bold personality.

People were also interested in Mr. Trump because they wanted to learn how to become rich and successful like him.

Mr. Trump also interested people because he frequently shared his strong opinions on topics like politics, government, international events, and world leaders.

Some people liked his straightforward style. Others were surprised and disturbed by provocative and sometimes unpopular things he said and did.

These varied public reactions made Mr. Trump a controversial figure. But people kept listening to hear his ideas and find out what he would do and say next.

> A **controversy** is when people have different opinions about a large, important, or public subject.

In 2015, Mr. Trump announced he would run for president as a member of the Republican Party.

A **political party** is a group of people who have similar ideas and usually vote for the same government leaders. The **Republican Party** is one of the major US parties. It is more than 160 years old!

Republicans are typically cautious about spending money. They think carefully about what to buy and how much things cost. They want us to earn more money than we spend, so we avoid debt.

If you borrow money, **debt** is the amount you owe and have to pay back.

Republicans usually favor a strong military, secure borders, and helping businesses create good American jobs. They want to keep people safe so everyone is free to work hard and build nice lives.

Mr. Trump's campaign slogan was "Make America Great Again." Many voters liked this idea from the start and supported Mr. Trump's platform.

A **slogan** is a phrase that describes a business or effort. A candidate's **platform** is his or her ideas about leading the country.

Mr. Trump's platform included strong ideas about how to protect Americans and keep them working in good jobs and businesses.

Unlike most presidential candidates, Mr. Trump had never been elected to a government job.

He had never worked for a city, state, or lawmaking organization.

The United States Congress is our federal **lawmaking body**. Its representatives and senators write and enact laws. Some former presidents, like President Barack Obama, were senators before they were president.

Some people thought a president should have experience working for the American people in an elected job.

However, many people just wanted a president who is smart and strong, and has good leadership experience.

They favored a president who can make good agreements, settle fights, have ideas, and share hope.

Some voters thought a good president should work to improve people's lives. Others believed a president's most important job is choosing a team of smart people to help him lead.

Mr. Trump and his supporters said his business success and experience proved he is a great leader with the knowledge and skills to be president.

Still, as a result of his political inexperience, many experts expected Mr. Trump's candidacy to fail.

When Mr. Trump entered the presidential race, 16 candidates were competing with him in the primary elections to become the Republican candidate.

The **primary** is the first phase of the presidential election. Voters choose which candidate will represent their party later in the national contest.

By Spring 2016, Mr. Trump had surprised many observers by winning more Republican primary votes than anyone else. His competitors quit.

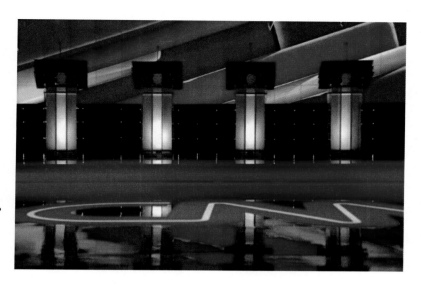

The July 2016 Republican National Convention made it official: Mr. Trump had earned the Republican nomination for president.

This meant that Mr. Trump's name would be on the official presidential ballot in the national election.

He would compete against former U.S. Secretary of State Hillary Clinton, the democratic party nominee, along with presidential candidates from smaller political parties.

The winner of that election would become the next president of the United States.

During the summer and fall of 2016, Mr. Trump and Secretary Clinton campaigned vigorously to defeat each other and win the votes of the American people.

They traveled all over the country, speaking to crowds about their ideas. They also met several times for lively debates that Americans watched on television.

The 2016 presidential race was close and exciting. Americans listened and waited for their day to vote.

When they finally went to the polls on election day November 8, 2016, no one knew who would win. Many people predicted that Secretary Clinton would receive more votes.

However, after a long and contentious campaign, Mr. Trump emerged as the winner.

He won millions of votes from people inspired by his message, ideas, and what they considered his potential to become a great national leader.

Secretary Clinton conceded the race.

As directed by the U.S. Constitution, President-elect Trump took the oath of office on Inauguration Day, January 20, 2017.

An **inauguration** is a ceremony that marks an official start. The U.S. Presidential Inauguration is a big event, where the new president promises to be a good president and obey the laws. This happens every four years on January 20th.

You ask, "Who is Donald J. Trump?"

He is the 45th president of the United States!

The End

Photographs

Updated for the 2020 Election!
Mommy, What is a Debate? draws children into the election conversation. With charming and hilarious animal photos, families can learn about debating, a most vital and visible component of modern elections. Read these fun, informative pages with your future voters, and engage them in the American democratic process.

MOMMY, WHAT IS A
DEBATE?

An Introduction to Debating for the 2020 Presidential Election

Taffy Jensen

http://www.vanaldenmedia.com/debate

Now an Amazon #1 Bestseller
Don't miss this introduction to President Trump's First Family. Because our youngest citizens are listening – and they have questions!

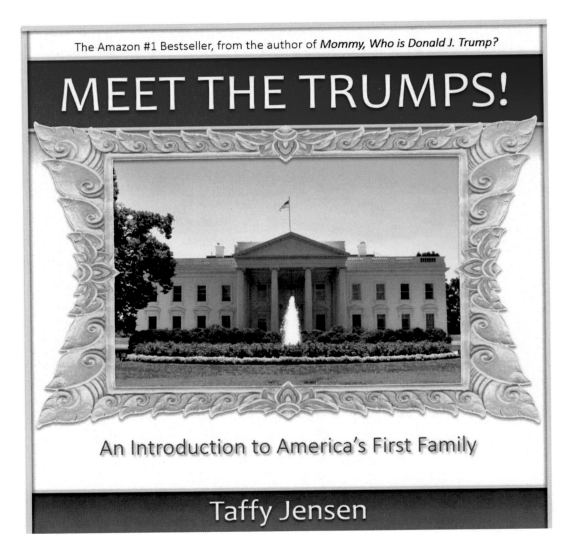

The Amazon #1 Bestseller, from the author of *Mommy, Who is Donald J. Trump?*

MEET THE TRUMPS!

An Introduction to America's First Family

Taffy Jensen

http://www.vanaldenmedia.com/mt

ABOUT THE AUTHOR

Taffy Jensen is an avid reader and, in her spare time, a mother of three active children. She writes about the questions her children ask. And they ask a LOT of questions.

Check out Taffy Jensen's other bestselling kids' learning books at www.vanaldenmedia.com.

Made in the USA
Las Vegas, NV
03 February 2025

17459170R00024